शब्दNama

A Journey Through Words

Divyanshi Gupta

BookLeaf Publishing
India | USA | UK

Made with ❤ on the BookLeaf Publishing Platform
www.bookleafpub.in
www.bookleafpub.com

Dedication

To my parents.

To the thirteen-year-old me, who unknowingly took the first step on this poetic journey.

To those who have walked beside me in silence and in song, your love and presence breathe life into my verses.

To the moments that stirred my soul, the words that found me, and the journey that shaped me.

And to the dreamers, the wanderers, and the lovers of words—may you find a part of yourself in these pages, just as I have found pieces of myself while writing them.

Preface

Poetry, for me, has always been more than *just* words—it is a reflection of what stirs the soul, what the eyes witness, and what the heart feels. Every poem in this collection is born from a moment—something I experienced, something I saw others go through, or something that was unfolding in the world around me.

There was no deliberate plan, no structured theme—just emotions seeking a voice. Some verses come from personal joys and sorrows, while others are echoes of stories left untold. In their own way, each poem is a fragment of life, a piece of memory, a thought that refused to be forgotten.

The title, "शब्दnama," represents this very journey—an anthology of words that carry meaning beyond what is written. This book is not just poetry; it is a conversation, a mirror, an experience shared.

I hope as you turn these pages, you find something that resonates with you, something that speaks to you in ways only poetry can.

Acknowledgements

This book is not just a collection of poems; it is a collection of moments—some lived, some observed, and some felt too deeply to ignore. Each verse carries echoes of emotions, fleeting thoughts, and unspoken words that found their way onto paper.

To those who have been a part of my journey, knowingly or unknowingly—you exist in these pages. Some of you may recognize a line, a feeling, or a memory woven between the words. While these poems were never written *for* anyone directly, they were often written *because of* someone. For that, I am grateful.

To my family and friends, your encouragement has been the silent force behind this book. To every reader who picks up these words and finds a reflection of their own story, thank you—for in your understanding, these poems find their true meaning.

And to poetry itself, for being the bridge between thoughts and expression, between the heart and the world.

The Weight Of A Name

The first thing you achieve at birth,
It is your identity on this earth.
Everyone calling out, low or loud,
That's what seperates you from the crowd.

Running hand in hand with the term fame,
A name that carries both glory and blame.
Something so simple, yet deeply profound,
Heavily confined yet endlessly unbound.

Let's not forget the surname, though;
It varies by gender, as we know.
Before marriage, she bears her maiden name;
Shouldn't it remain constant, not a shifting game?

There is a cultural divide, the name is observed,
Love fails, people part, and society is preserved.
Does it truly shape our true identity,
Or does it restrict our individuality?

"What's in a name?" is often said,
The grand scheme, existing beyond one, is dead.
What should shine—the human or the name?
Or is it just a plot for social blame and the survivorship game?

Conditions Apply

A tap on the shoulder, and I take a pause,
"What, in your view, is the one of world's biggest flaws?"
"Oh, that's a big one—where do I start?
And should I employ my mind or my heart?"

"Go for higher education, learn to compete,
There's nothing in the world a girl can't beat."
"You look so pretty—are you sure you belong?
I'll help you rise, but don't take too long..."

"It's late tonight; I have work to prepare,"
"Why do you bother? Just stay home and care!"
"I'm so proud—you led the discussion today!"
"But can you cook? How will you manage your stay?"

"Study harder, chase success, make us all proud,
But don't take too long—your wedding has been vowed."
"Be strong, be fierce, carve out your way,
But don't gain weight—you must look okay!"

A tap on the shoulder, and I take a pause,
A lifetime of rules, yet I am the cause?
I smile, I nod, I play along,
But in my heart, I *know* they're wrong.

Balance it all, that's the ultimate motive.
Be the perfect partner, the mother, the devotive,
But don't lose yourself, keep it all inside.
Be strong, be soft, but don't dare collide.

Confessions Of A Serial Snoozer

Making bold plans to wake up early,
Setting alarms- arranged so thoroughly.
Screen flashing, buzzing every two minutes,
How many are too many? There are no limits.

And just like that, the first beep rings,
Mornings are when sleep tightly clings.
Blaming myself for the endless disturbance,
Forgetting *'who'* set this chain into occurrence.

The quilt holds me in its warm embrace,
I still see stars, though the sun lights up space.
"Not again," I sigh at my alarm's chime,
Knowing it'll steal my peace in no time.

Tucked my phone beneath my pillow,
The buzzing, now a bit mellow.
"Are you dozing off again?"—
My subconscious mind warned, like fate ordained.

The final buzz—eyes strained to the time,
Squinting hard, as if stung by lime!
Oh no, I overslept once more and longer,
What will you call me a serial snoozer—or a lazymonger?

Fading Silhouettes

One morning, looking at the children's park,
An observation roared, rather stark.
When all the complaints were so timid,
Childhood was the best phase and most vivid.

Waiting for weekends to savour Maggi and gulp it all,
Now, it's just quick meals— no time to enjoy, big or small.
From making paper boats to jumping on rain puddles,
To curing allergies and craving cuddles.

"I will play first," fighting over the bat—neon and of plastic,
Popping the bubble wrap becomes nostalgic.
Making temporary homes from leftover cardboard,
Now chasing dreams that we can barely afford.

Sitting with parents each evening and talking about school,
Calling them on video calls, and being an urban fool.

From knowing neighbours and playing hand in hand,
To friending them on Instagram and leaving messages unplanned.

And yet, in the rush to grow, we lost the art,
Of living in moments, of holding a heart.
Now we race to succeed, but forget to reflect,
The simple joys we used to collect.

घर चौबारे की गूंज

"चलो तुमको कल गाँव हैं ले चलते,
जहाँ मेरा बचपन बीता, जहाँ सुविचार हैं पलते।"
"गाँव में ऐसा क्या है, जिसका आपके शब्द करें घेरा"
"अरे बेटा, घर तो तब था, अब तो बस है बसेरा।"

"जब हर सुबह, हर आंगन में पंचायत थी बैठ जाती,
हंसी-ठिठोली से दीवारें भी खिलखिलाती।
हर दिन किसी त्योहार से कम नहीं था लगता,
जितने ज्यादा सदस्य, उतना घर में दम था भरता।

अब "परिवार" शब्द के मायने बदलते जा रहे,
कोई समझाए अगर, तो कहाँ कोई शांति से कुछ सहे?
पहले घर का मुखिया सूरज जैसा था उगता,
अब त्योहारों, समारोह में मिलना भी बंधक-सा लगता।

अब संबंधों में मूल्य नहीं, सब स्वार्थ में हैं बंटे,
दरवाज़े तो बड़े हो गए, दिल हुए और छोटे।
अपनों से घृणा में नजरें रखते हैं जैसे हों गिद्ध,
घर का जोगी जोगना, आन गाँव का सिद्ध।

जैसे पुराने ज़माने के गीतों में हुआ करता था अर्थ,
और आज की ऊँची ध्वनि में सब कुछ लगे निरर्थ।
वैसे ही पहले रिश्तों की गहराई कभी नापनी नहीं पड़ी,
एक पर उँगली उठी, तो सारी रिश्तेदारियाँ मुट्ठी बन होती थीं खड़ी!

अब कोई अपनों से नहीं जुड़ा, सब में है अपना स्वार्थ,
जितना लिया, उतना बढ़ा, रिश्ते भी अब नहीं हैं साथ।
अब बस यादों में ही वो चौपालें मिलीं,
दिलों के रिश्तों की रस्सियाँ ढीली सी हो चलीं।

The Cycle Of News

Breaking news flashes right up on the screen,
And just like that, we watch with our eyes keen.
A big celebrity *apparently* took their own life,
We focus on the headlines, forgetting our strife.

"Oh, it's so tragic! Why does this persist?"
"But by the evening, it won't even exist."
Then my mind stirs, a thought takes hold—
Are we desensitized, too numb to be bold?

News flash—rapes reported with frightening ease,
Wars waged for land, as greed won't cease.
Markets crash, leaving people in pain,
Fires sweep with rage, and only ruins remain.

Political clashes, riots unfold,
Yet it's the people like us left out in the cold.
But what can people like us really do?
We sit on our couches and follow it through.

Is there a way to break this chain,
To see beyond the scripted frame?
Why do we trust what they choose to show,
When some truth is buried deep below?

And if we stop, choose not to see,
Are we blind, or are we free?
For if we don't care, if we don't react,
Who will question? Who will act?

In The Eyes Of A Stranger

Walking through the crowd, surrounded by strangers,
Not catching the metro or being pushed—just imagined dangers.
The escalators run at maximum capacity,
The sheer volume they carry fills me with pity.

I reach my station, waiting for my train,
People stand in a messy queue, drenched in sweat and strain.
I board the metro, with not a single seat spare,
Leaning by the pole, time passes without a care.

I take a glance around, just to observe,
A young girl stares at her phone, smiling with every nerve.
"She must be texting someone special," I assume with a grin,
Delusional or am I just too lost within?

Beside her, a mother feeds her child with care,

The kid plays with a ball, while I simply stare.
I shift my gaze to an old woman nearby,
Knitting a sweater, humming blessings with a sigh.

I watch, I wonder, as moments unfold,
How many stories remain untold?
Do they see me as *just* another face?
A fleeting presence, gone without a trace?

Perhaps the girl wasn't texting someone dear,
Just scrolling through memories that bring her near.
Maybe the mother, though gentle in sight,
Hides a storm she dares not to fight.

The old woman's chants—are they prayers or pain?
Does she knit warmth or stitch through disdain?
How little I know, yet how much I presume,
As if glances alone can dismiss the gloom.

Strangers we are, strangers we'll be,
Passing like shadows, too blind to see.
In a world where our stories rarely entwine,
Do we exist to each other or just in our mind?

Mind Games

"You are running again," I said to my mind,
Calling my thoughts out—they aren't being kind.
"Oh, I'm just calculating your next step!"
"We both know you need extra prep."

"Look at you mocking me!" I exclaimed.
"It's all your doing, yet I am the one being framed."
"Why do you tangle me in your designs?"
"And twist my thoughts like creeping vines!"

"I do this to keep you cautious, my love," mind mutters.
"I know you well—your heart often flutters."
"But aren't there greater worries to unwind?"
I ask, a quiet plea in my mind.

"So you want me to think even more?"
"Are there any avenues left to explore?"
The mind just chuckles, whispering instead
"You fuel my engine, I drive ahead."

I sigh and wonder, is this a game?
A cycle of doubt, always the same.
No finish line, no end in sight,
Just racing thoughts in endless flight.

Suddenly, I wake with a jolt and a shock,
Was I overthinking? Was that the knock?
I love myself dearly, but will this ever stop?
Oh, my mind will always use me as a prop!

Who Stays, Who Fades

"What are your plans for your birthday?
Let me know, if you'd like me to invite someone your way?"
"Actually everyone is occupied with something of their own,
It's disheartening, but maybe that was always known."

"They show up in pictures, in stories and in cheer,
But vanish when presence is needed to be near.
What does real friendship really feel like?
Does it stay, or fade like a passing strike?

Oh, real friendship is like a steady flame,
Through storms and sunshine, it stays the same.
You laugh, you cry and share without fear,
It's love in its purest, unwavering sphere.

Whether you talk daily or take months apart,
It never leaves a grudge in the heart.
A friend who listens and will never betray,

Who stands by your side, come what may.

But lately, the world has taken a turn,
True connections are fading, cause to discern.
Belittling in whispers, yet walking in packs,
Smiles in the front, with knives at the backs.

So how do you tell who's false, who's true?
Is there a test that real friends must pass through?
Perhaps it's in silence, in time, in space,
The ones who remain are the ones you embrace.

Not only in the moments of laughter and glee,
But in shadows, in storms, in vulnerability.
A friend is not just a name in your phone,
But the one who reminds you—you're never alone."

अहम से अंत तक

कौन कहता है कि तुम सतयुगी बन जाओ,
किसी तरह थोड़ी उदारता तो अपने में ले आओ।
अरे, नहीं स्वीकारनी अगर कोई बात,
तो कम से कम शब्दों से मत तोड़ो किसी के जज़्बात।

क्या उपलब्धि है आख़िर तुम्हारी?
यही कि ईश्वर ने बना दिया तुम्हें नर-नारी?
अगर उसने बनाया है, तो क्या मिटाएगा नहीं?
तो तुम्हें कैसे पता कि तुम्हारा आचरण है सही?

क्यों अपने रोष में भूल जाता मनुष्य प्रकृति का नियम,
एक ही जिंदगी मिली है, क्यों ना सुधारें अपने कर्म?
हाँ, माना कि यह कविता ज्ञान दे रही,
कर लो संशोधन—अभी तो गंगा बह रही...

पर सोचो, जब यह धारा भी जाएगी रुक,
हर सीख, हर चेतावनी व्यर्थ हो जाएगी जैसे झुक।
बचेगा बस अहंकार, कुछ भूले-बिसरे नाम,
फिर ढूंढोगे सतयुग, पर न होगा कोई धाम।

Unfinished Conversations

They come like a cold night breeze,
Wrap around you, filling you with ease.
Yet moving forward brings endless doubt,
You scream, you whisper—but none hear you out.

They feel so right, unlike the cruelty of time,
To hold that love back almost seems a crime.
They stay within, a place set apart—
Never gone, just waiting in your heart.

A bond so strong, yet left incomplete,
You laugh at the irony, but it's bittersweet.
Who said it always has to last?
When the person is right, time runs too fast.

Then comes this void, silent yet loud—
A piece of you lost in the lingering shroud.
As if a spell was quietly cast,
A love untouched, forever to last.

Echoes Of Fear

How to define fear, I randomly thought,
How can it exist, something never sought?
More strangely, how one actually discovers,
What is it that actually gives the shivers?

Why doesn't anyone talk about the intangible?
What the mind believes it to be inevitable.
Some have the fear of loneliness,
The within one is more than the real darkness.

It wears many masks, it shifts its form,
Sometimes a whisper, sometimes a storm.
A step too far, a path unknown,
A quiet ache when you're alone.

Is it the past that never fades,
Or the future wrapped in silent shades?
What lies within, what lies outside,
Which one is real, which one just hides?

Letter To Younger Self

Ever wondered what would happen if you knew?
Wouldn't your actions be set and aligned in a queue?
But life and time don't work like that,
Unforeseen circumstances often come to chat!

My thirteen-year-old self was the first to write,
Never did she know what would become her life's highlight.
The naive, beautiful young girl, her movements were precisioned,
She thought she would live just as she envisioned.

The warm-hearted girl, with many calling her *best friend*,
Heartbroken when most of those bonds had to end.
She believed the greatest strength was the ability to be vulnerable,
Thinking she'd find the perfect man, suitable!

It's been tough for her, in this ever-changing world,

Careers switched, friendships lost, emotions unfurled.
Winning battles and rising at every level,
Knocking them down when life threw its pebble.

Whose life has been easy, you may say,
But look at her now, standing strong in *her* way.
She's learned through the years, with wisdom to show,
The core values stay, as she continues to grow.

And now she knows, with clarity so bright,
That life's true strength is in embracing the fight.
No matter the challenges, no matter the cost,
The journey's been worth it, no lessons lost.

Muted In Reality, Viral Online

"Which one should be the first picture to get posted?",
she asked,
He sighed, took his phone, and left—his escape
unmasked.
"Yes, leave, why would you ever be of any aid?
Held her phone, placed cushions and down she laid.

In seconds, his phone buzzed, lighting up the screen,
Tagged in her post—a picture-perfect scene.
The caption stated - 'choosing you over everything',
Yet their reality was unravelling, tied by a string.

Smiles framed in pixels and memories written in gold,
Yet in real conversations, it's distant and cold.
We meet to click, we talk to trend,
But where's the warmth we used to send?

Hearts and likes flow like a fleeting cheer,
Yet silence lingers around loud and clear.

Flawless filters, picture-perfect nights,
Yet unread texts hide the unseen fights.

Crowd beneath posts, but solitude within,
Validation screams, but voices stay thin.
Typing... deleting... rethinking replies,
Behind curated joy, the real us dies.

If presence is measured in stories and tags,
Then why do emotions feel like lifeless rags?
If love is seen *but* never heard,
Are we connected, or just blurred?

शक्ति और सवाल

सब जानते हैं क्या है असलियत,
पर अनजान बने रहने की है नीयत।
क्यों क़ाबू में कर लड़कियों को रोकते,
पर जंगली दरिंदों को नहीं हैं टोकते?

नारी जब अपनी बात कहे तो वो तेज़, जवाबी कहलायी,
पर ऐसी रुकावट मर्दों ने कब सही।
अगर पुरुष होना उनकी है विजय,
तो उसको जन्म देने वाली शक्ति है अजय।

शरीर ढका हो या हो नन्ही सी जान,
कुछ आदमी दानवों से भी बड़े हैवान।
आख़िर क्यों नहीं सिखाया सबको इज़्ज़त देना?
हर नारी को इंसान समझकर देखना?

क्या होगा अगर बदल गया क़ानून?
क्या हैवानियत बदल लेगी अपना खून?
ख़ुद को बदलो, लाओ बदलाव की लहर निराली,
इससे पहले कि हर नारी बन जाए प्रचंड माँ काली।

When Nature Took A Pause

I close my eyes in self-isolation from Corona,
And I see a vast yet idle arena.
A bird chirped constantly on one side,
Fluttering freely, with no need to hide.

Isn't it plausible to suggest,
That our freedom came at their behest?
Who said only humans have the right to stroll?
Is nature truly under man's control?

Suddenly, my eyes opened wide—
Had nature simply switched its side?
No wonder the times are harsh and tough,
Perhaps the world needed a break, and this is all a bluff?

This thought brought a tender smile,
For Mother Nature, it's best we stay immobile.
After all, adversity and loss make a man wise,
And I wonder— is isolation a blessing in disguise?

Rebooting Life

Yes, after pandemic life was at a halt,
Was it truly someone's fault?
Or did we arrive here by our own design,
Believing we were prime, with nature merely a sign?

Nothing—and yet so much has changed,
How do we reboot? I remain engaged.
Stagnant yet functional, the world spun around,
While inner peace was lost, then found.

The echoes of stillness whisper near,
Fading doubts, dissolving fear.
A canvas blank, a story untold,
Step ahead—let life unfold.

Oh, hello! The dawdling time has ticked away,
Pick up your brushes—paint a new day.
Buckled up, with laces tied,
Mere existence will now stride.

Let's Change The Topic

Let’s talk about depression.
Indescribable?
Can you define it, though?
Is it the same for you?

No, it’s not that I cry randomly,
I laugh when I think I should.
No, I don’t starve,
I eat when I think I should.

No, I am not alone,
I am surrounded by people.
They talk to me,
And I answer them back.

Thoughts linger longer,
Solutions seem farther,
Uncertainties run parallel,
Anxiety becomes familiar.

But does something still feel insufficient?
Is it within me?
Do you sense it too?
Or am I overanalyzing again?

Let's change the topic.
Maybe I'm wrong.
Or maybe I'm not?
Is it the same for you?

The Solace Within

At the end, I'm my own comfort,
Songs play all day, but in the mirror, I find my concert.
Some hear, some overhear, but none truly listen,
Explaining myself gives the desired glisten.

My thoughts reside only within me,
So why must others always agree?
The only care and keeping I truly own,
It's a selfish world out there—a fact well known.

Not all echoes need a reply,
Some truths shine brightest in a silent sky.
If the world won't listen, let it be,
For I am enough—whole and free.

Love yourself and let go, I assert,
For in the end, I'm my own comfort.

गुमशुदा रास्तों पर

अब अपने घर को है जाना,
अनजान शहर में कब तक दिखे ठिकाना,
माना रोटी है यहाँ कमायी,
पर जान तो गाँव में है सदा बसायी,
अब गुमशुदा रास्तों पर पैदल है अपनी चढ़ाई ।

"नहीं बापू, अब नहीं चला जा रहा",
आठ साल की पिंकी ने दुखी मन से कहा,
"तुम गोद में उठा लो हमें",
अपने झुके काँधे पर रख, बिना थमे...
गुमशुदा रास्तों पर पैदल ही फिर बढ़ चले ।

यह कौन से रास्ते बार-बार मिल रहे,
ठंडी रेत तो कभी गरम पत्थर चोट को सहे,
कभी तेज़ रफ़्तार से कदम बढ़े,
तो कभी थकान में सुस्त पड़े,
अब गुमशुदा रास्तों पर पैदल ही बढ़ चले ।

भूख तो बड़ी लगी है,
चार दिन पुरानी रोटी साथ में पड़ी है,

पिंकी की माँ सबके लिए बना लाई,
अब सूखे कौर से कर लेंगे पूरी चढ़ाई,
गुमशुदा रास्तों पर पैदल चलने की लड़ाई।

अब अपने गाँव की सड़क ही है किनारा,
वहीं तालाब का पानी होगा प्यास का सहारा।
बस घर की दिशा में अग्रसर होना है काम,
वो आम के पेड़ के तले ही मिलेगा आराम,
गुमशुदा रास्तों पर बस चलना, नहीं कोई विराम।

रिश्तों का बदलता मौसम

मन करता मनमानी, अपनी मनवाने की ठानी,
कोई समझे होशियारी, कोई कहे बेमानी।
पर कौन ग़लत और कौन सही?
इसका उत्तर क्या छुपा है कहीं?

क्यों अब अपनी ही सोच लगती सबसे उचित?
क्या और कोई नहीं चाहता हमारा हित?
सोचो तो चारों ओर इंसान ही दिखते,
पर अपने खोजने पर भी नहीं मिलते...

अपनों से बात करने से पहले क्यों मन को टटोलते?
क्या अब रिश्तों के मोल कहीं बिकते?
जब कोई सगा भी सगा सा ना रहे,
तो दिल के ज़ख़्म अब किससे कहें?

आख़िर मन ठहरकर बस इतना ही बोल पाए...
"अब जो हो, राम ही पार लगाए।"

When Love Slips Away

What happened to my affinity,
When forever was tied to serendipity.
When you and I, apart, never existed,
How come now everything feels so twisted?

The dark nights grew unnervingly darker,
And the pain of tears cut even sharper.
You became a meteor, but I longed for a star,
When I needed you most, you were far.

Was that hand, once held, just temporary?
Still, that memory remains unsworn and not blurry.
Are you alright, so distant and far away,
With my absence haunting you every day?

I thought love was meant to stay,
But it slipped like dusk to grey.
Did we lose what we had, or did it fade away?
Now I search for your face, but find only dismay.

Can we ever reconcile,
Though apart by a thousand mile?
Then, would we be happy together?
Or is it true—now, the farther, the better.

In The Grip Of Technology

"What does that word mean, the one we played in
scrabble?
Were you actually right, or I am just probable."
"Wait, let me check the meaning real quick,
Can't you let me enjoy my win for a bit?"

The internet connectivity was suddenly lost,
This lapse was frustrating, creating mental exhaust.
How even simple words now require online validation,
Oh, this omnipresent screen intelligence—what an
innovation!

With one click, the world seems under your finger,
Everything's under control, no mind-memory ringer!
Have we lost our ability to act, to think without
assistance ?
Or is there an illusion of brilliance in this existence?

But as the saying goes, for every rose there's a thorn,
Was life once simpler, before internet was born?

There was no instant connection, no virtual sensation,
But now we have better defense, medical and communication.

Yet dependence grows, as we let the screen guide our way,
Reaching for answers, we don't think or delay.
A boon and bane, technology in our hands,
It shapes our world, but also makes us less than we planned.

ख़ामोश उम्मीदें

कुछ सोचकर हम चुप रहे,
मायूस थे, पर सह गए।
पर कर रहा था दिल-दिमाग़ सवाल,
सिर्फ़ मैं समझूँ? यही था ख़याल।

आख़िर तुम क्यूँ नहीं पूछते,
कभी मेरी सुध नहीं बूझते ।
कभी मैं भी बताना चाहती अपनी बातें,
साथ हैं, पर जैसे तन्हा कटती हैं रातें ।

अगर सब एक, तो दर्द क्यूँ बँटा हुआ ?
अपना हाल बताना चाहता है मेरा रुवां रुवां ।
कब तक एक तरफ़ा डोर खिचेगा,
यह रिश्ता आख़िर कब तक बचेगा ?

एक दूजे को समझने का था वादा,
तुम्हारे लिए रंग पर मेरे लिए सब सादा ।
उम्मीद है, अब तुम समझ गए मुझे,
बस इस ख़्याल से खिल गए जो दिए थे बुझे ।

"आज नहीं, कल पक्का" तुम फिर कहे,
कुछ सोच कर हम चुप रहे...

Whispers Of The Woods

Wandering in the woods,
Away from men and worldly goods.
A few steps toward self-recognition,
And some away from life's decisions.

The leaves whisper as silent audience,
The path glows with a guiding radiance.
Tropical waters hum a tune so bright,
While twigs crackle in golden light.

None to disturb this tranquil space,
None to outrun in life's endless race.
The sun wraps me in a warm embrace,
And the wind hums with soothing grace.

If such peace exists, why cut the trees?
Why trade fresh air for tainted ease?
Respect nature, let it stand tall,
Or we shall crumble with its fall.